W9-ATB-104

LUNGS

YOUR RESPIRATORY SYSTEM

SEYMOUR SIMON

🌐 Smithsonian | ⚬ Collins

An Imprint of HarperCollinsPublishers

PICTURE CREDITS

page 4: Véronique Estiot / Photo Researchers, Inc.; page 7: Mehau Kulyk / Photo Researchers, Inc.; page 8: John Bavosi / Photo Researchers, Inc.; inset: Susumu Nishinaga / Photo Researchers, Inc.; page 11: VEM / Photo Researchers, Inc.; inset: CNRI / Photo Researchers, Inc.; page 12: Innerspace Imaging / Photo Researchers, Inc.; page 15: Zephyr / Photo Researchers, Inc.; inset: J. Bavosi / Photo Researchers, Inc.; page 16: Sellem-Demri-Voisin / Photo Researchers, Inc.; page 19: Science Photo Library / Photo Researchers, Inc.; page 20: Lea Paterson / Photo Researchers, Inc.; pages 23, 27: Kent Wood / Photo Researchers, Inc.; page 24: Mark Clark / Photo Researchers, Inc.; page 28: LADA / Photo Researchers, Inc.; inset: CNRI / Photo Researchers, Inc.; page 31: Coneyl Jay / Photo Researchers, Inc.

The name of the Smithsonian, Smithsonian Institution and the sunburst logo
are registered trademarks of the Smithsonian Institution.
Collins is an imprint of HarperCollins Publishers.

Library of Congress Cataloging-in-Publication Data
Simon, Seymour.
    Lungs / Seymour Simon.— 1st ed.
        p.   cm.
    Includes bibliographical references and index.
    ISBN-10: 0-06-054654-9 (trade bdg.) — ISBN-13: 978-0-06-054654-0 (trade bdg.)
    ISBN-10: 0-06-054655-7 (lib. bdg.) — ISBN-13: 978-0-06-054655-7 (lib. bdg.)
    1. Lungs—Juvenile literature. 2. Respiration—Juvenile literature. I. Title.
QP121.S553 2007   2006003768
612.2—dc22
Typography by Drew Willis
1 2 3 4 5 6 7 8 9 10
❖
First Edition

Smithsonian Mission Statement

For more than 160 years, the Smithsonian has remained true to its mission, "the increase and diffusion of knowledge." Today the Smithsonian is not only the world's largest provider of museum experiences supported by authoritative scholarship in science, history, and the arts but also an international leader in scientific research and exploration. The Smithsonian offers the world a picture of America, and America a picture of the world.

Introduction

Did you know that you breathe more than 20,000 times each and every day? Your lungs provide this amazing service, day in and day out, along with many other important activities that we simply take for granted. Read on to discover why your lungs are at work every time you speak, play a musical instrument, smell cookies baking, yawn, snore, sneeze, cough, or hiccup. How do they do it? The answers are here, providing details on how your entire respiratory system functions, and explaining why your lungs are so important. From the moment you are born, your lungs are on the job, making everything else you do possible.

—Don E. Wilson
Senior Scientist and Curator of Mammals
National Museum of Natural History
Smithsonian Institution

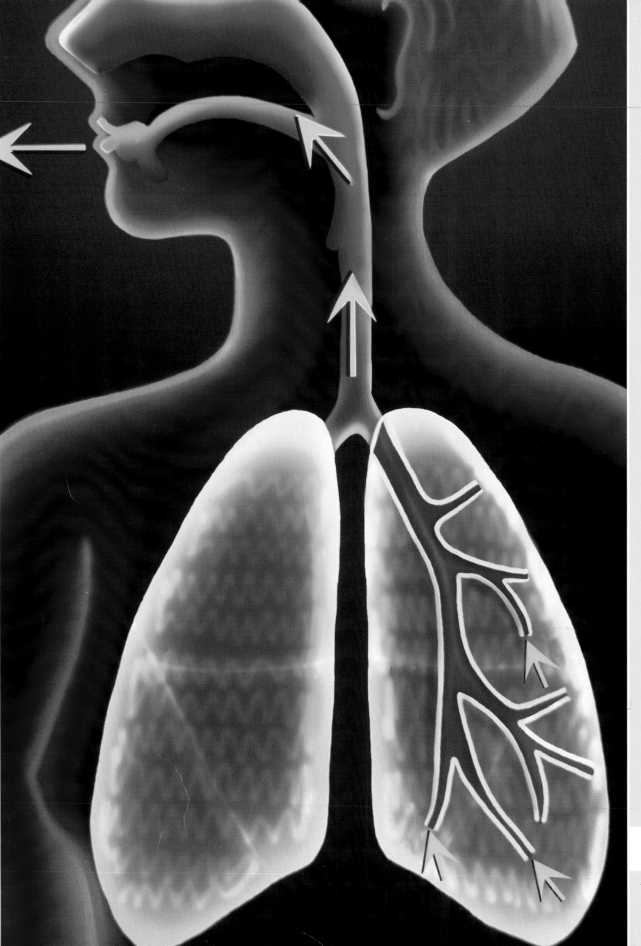

Flow of exhaled carbon dioxide

Take a deep breath and hold it for as long as you can. Use the second hand of a watch to time yourself. You may be surprised to find that you have to take a breath before a minute or two has passed. Humans may be able to go for days without food or water, but we can live for only a few minutes without air.

You live at the bottom of a layer of air called the atmosphere. Earth's atmosphere contains oxygen, the gas you need to get energy from the foods you eat, fuel your muscles, keep your heart pumping, and perform many other important functions for your survival. When you breathe in, or inhale, oxygen rushes into your body. When you breathe out, or exhale, you get rid of a waste gas called carbon dioxide.

Your lungs and the other parts of your respiratory system allow you to inhale and exhale, to speak and make noises with your mouth, to blow up a balloon, and to play a trumpet or a flute. Awake or asleep, you breathe in and out every minute of every hour, of every day, of every year for your entire life.

The journey of air to your lungs begins when you inhale through your nose or mouth. Your nose is made up of a strong, flexible substance called **cartilage**. A piece of cartilage divides your nose into two nostrils. The insides of the nostrils are lined with tiny hairs called cilia that help to filter the air and trap dust particles.

The nostrils open into a space called the nasal cavity. The walls of the nasal cavity produce a moist, sticky material called **mucus**. Mucus traps germs and bits of dust that get past the nostrils. Mucus also helps warm and moisten the air you breathe. Tear ducts from your eyes lead into the nasal cavity. When you cry, tears roll down your face and also drain into the nasal cavity. That's why your nose "runs" when you cry.

Sinuses are air spaces in the skull that are linked to the nasal cavity. Sometimes sinuses become infected or swell up because of an allergy to pollen, dust, or other substances. You feel congested and may get a headache. Steam or a humidifier can help relieve the pressure of sinus congestion.

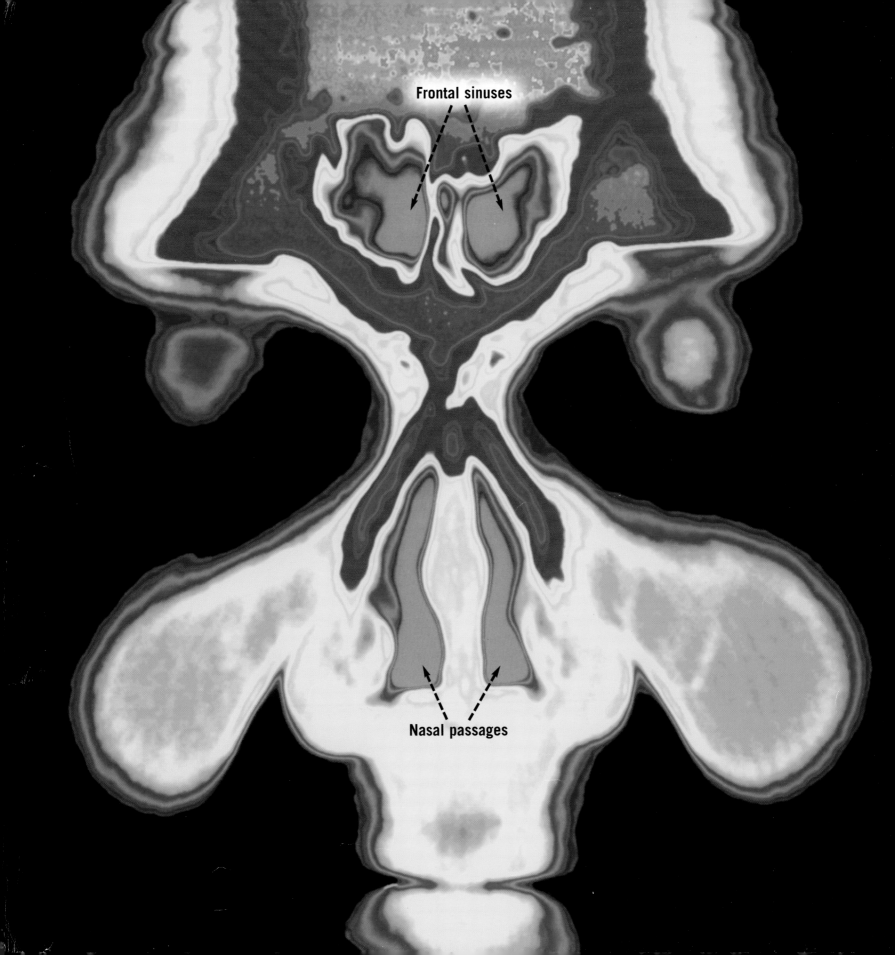

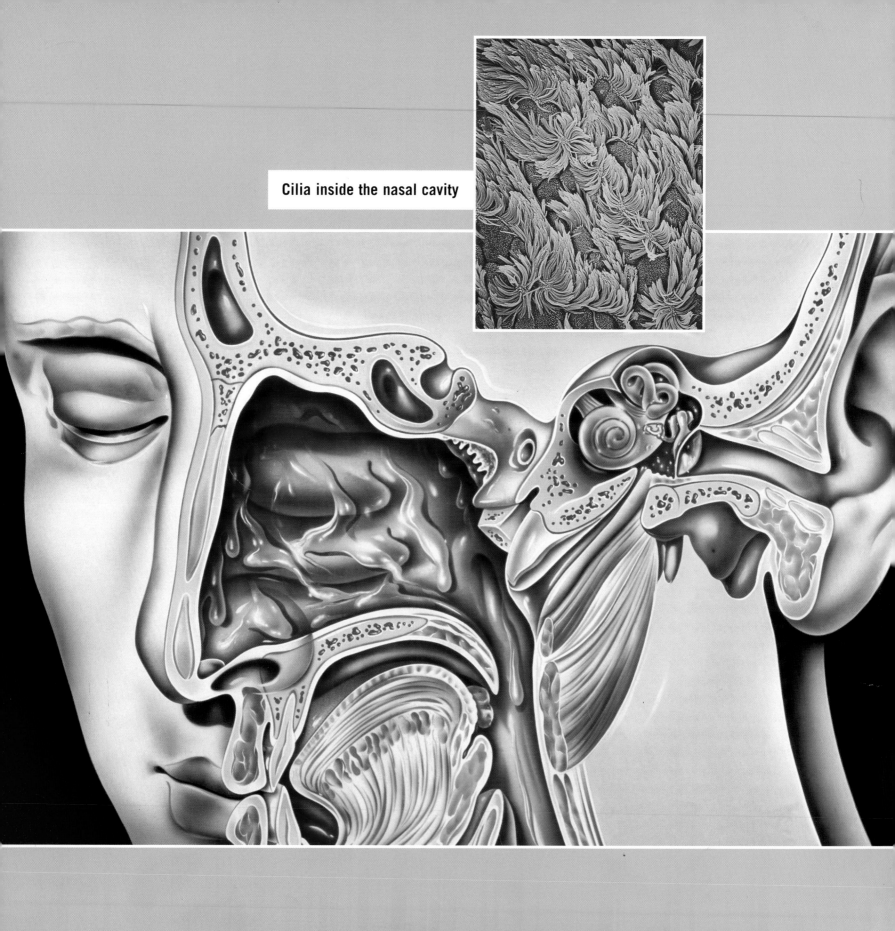

Cilia inside the nasal cavity

At the top of the nasal cavity are two thumbnail-sized spots called the olfactory centers. (*Olfactory* means "relating to smell.") Olfactory **cells** are very tiny. There are about fifty million in your nose. (A dog's nose has two billion odor receptors, many more than your nose has.) There are hundreds of different kinds of odor receptors; each can sense only one kind of odor. A smell is sensed by a few different odor receptors.

Cilia stick out from the olfactory cells in your nose. The cilia wave back and forth like grass in the wind. They respond to chemicals in the air and send signals to the olfactory centers. The centers organize the signals into patterns. Your brain interprets the patterns as different smells.

Humans can distinguish about ten thousand different smells. Your brain learns to tell one from another very quickly. Your sense of smell can help to keep you safe. For example, the smell of something burning can alert you to a fire before you see it.

After passing through your nasal cavity, air travels into your throat, or pharynx. The pharynx is a muscular tube lined with mucus that starts behind the nose and stretches down about five inches through the neck. The air tube leading to your lungs has a small flap called the epiglottis. The flap opens when you breathe air but closes when you swallow food. If you try to do both at the same time, you may start to choke. That's what can happen if you laugh while drinking water or cough while swallowing food.

Your larynx, or voice box, is located at the bottom of the pharynx. The front and side walls of the box are sometimes called your Adam's apple.

Two thin folds of tissue stretch across your voice box. These are your vocal cords. When you breathe, the cords relax and allow air to pass through easily. When you speak or sing, tiny muscles stretch the vocal cords tightly. Air pushed out of your lungs makes the cords move back and forth quickly. The rapid movements, or vibrations, make a sound. Just like a plucked rubber band, the tighter the cords are stretched, the higher pitched the sound they produce.

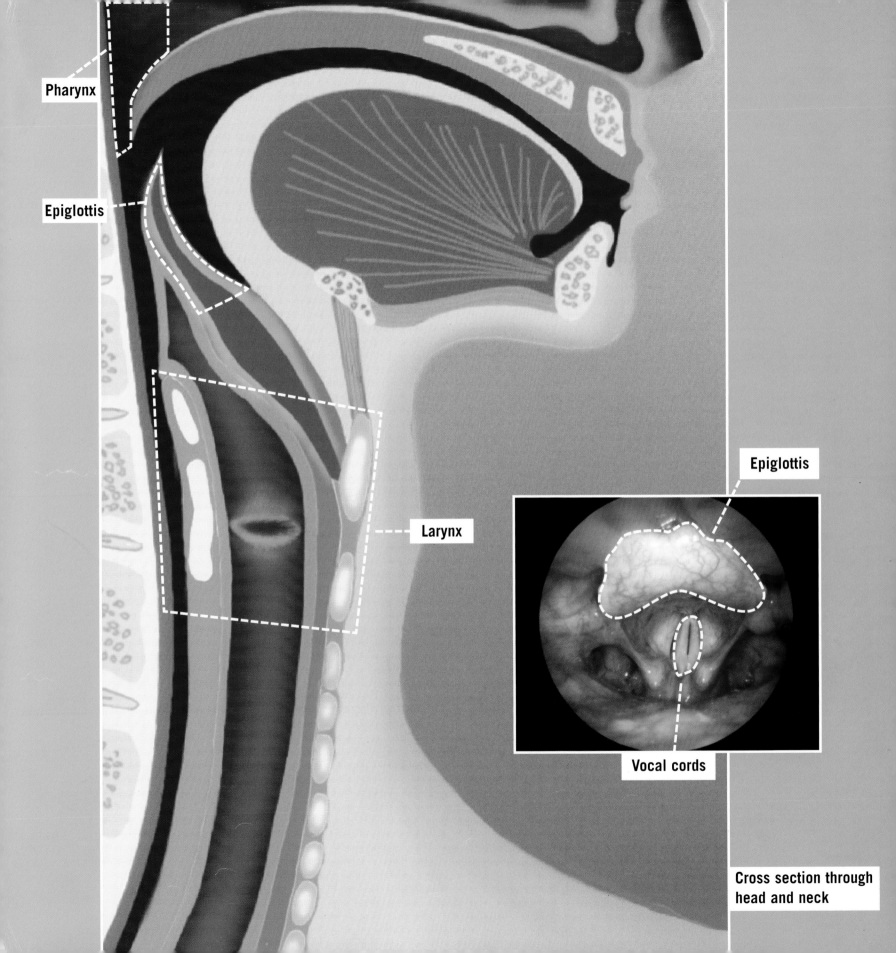

Pharynx

Epiglottis

Larynx

Epiglottis

Vocal cords

Cross section through head and neck

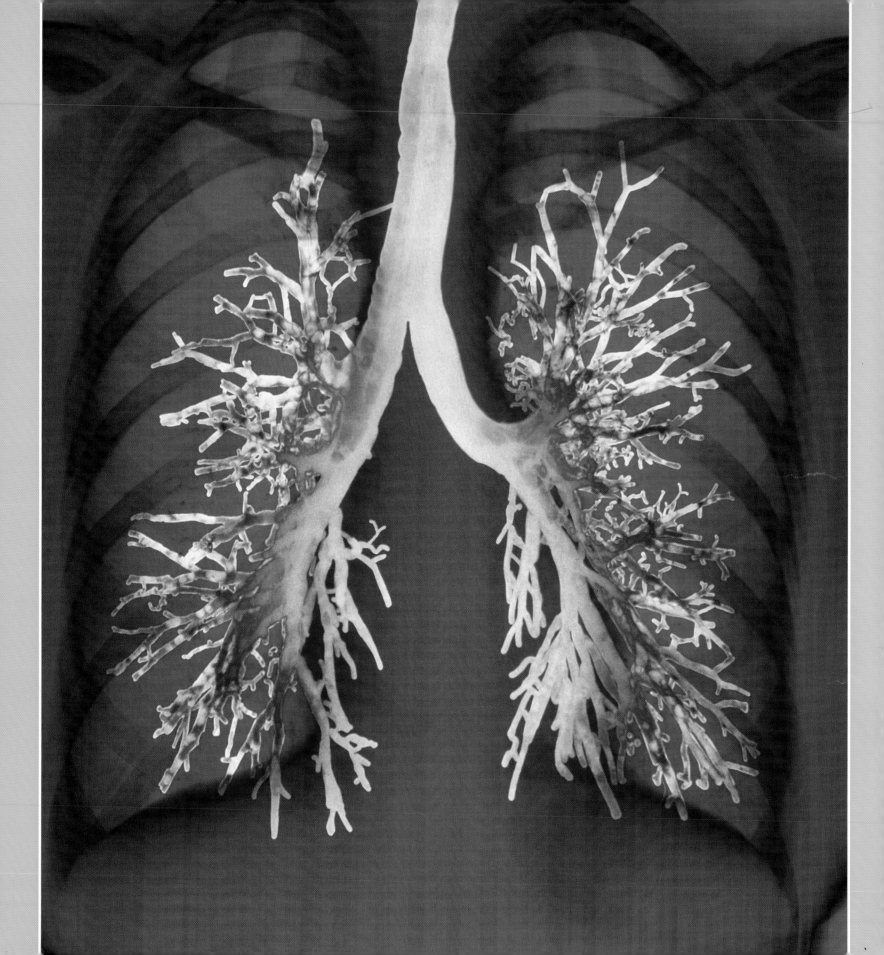

Below your voice box air moves into the windpipe, or trachea. Place your fingers against the lower part of your neck. You can feel the rings of stiff cartilage that form the walls of the trachea. The rings are connected by muscles, which allow you to bend and stretch and still keep your windpipe open.

Toward the middle of your chest, the trachea splits into two narrower tubes called the bronchi. One tube leads into the right lung and the other into the left lung. Each bronchus splits into smaller and smaller bronchial tubes that look like the branches on a tree. Finally, each tiny air tube ends in a little bunch of air sacs called **alveoli**.

Your lungs contain more than six hundred million alveoli. The bunches look like clusters of grapes. You would need a microscope to see a single one. However, if all the tiny alveoli were spread out flat, they would cover a much larger surface than your entire skin.

A network of small blood vessels called **capillaries** surrounds each air sac. The walls, or **membranes**, of the alveoli and the capillaries are very thin and close to one another. **Molecules** of oxygen and carbon dioxide can pass through the walls in either direction.

In a process called diffusion, substances move from an area of high concentration to an area of lower concentration. When you inhale, the air that travels to the alveoli has a large amount of oxygen in it. The blood in the capillaries traveling from the heart has a small amount of oxygen. This means that many oxygen molecules diffuse through the alveoli and capillary walls and into the blood. Oxygen is picked up by a substance in the red blood cells called **hemoglobin**. Blood, now rich in oxygen, is carried back to the heart, where it is pumped to all the cells of the body.

At the same time, carbon dioxide molecules diffuse through the capillary and alveoli walls into the alveoli. When you exhale, you give off carbon dioxide into the air.

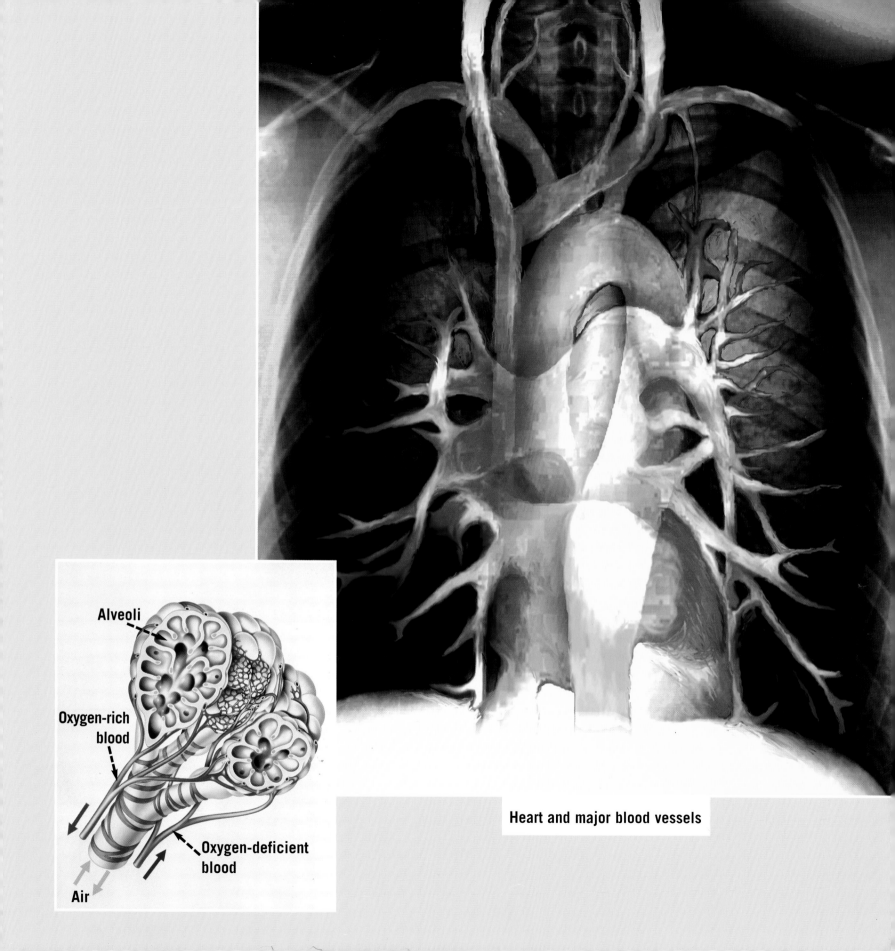

Alveoli

Oxygen-rich blood

Oxygen-deficient blood

Air

Heart and major blood vessels

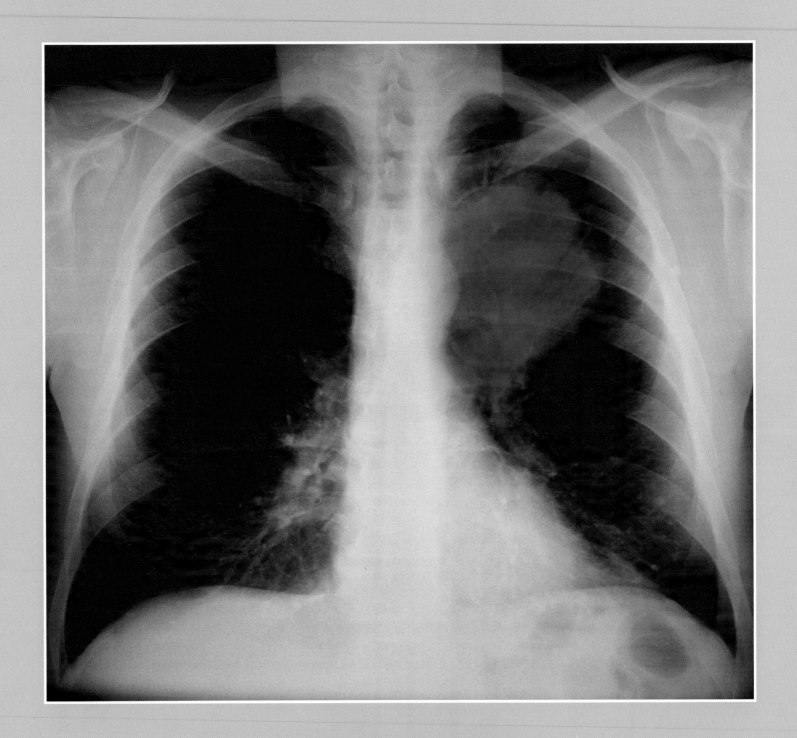

Your lungs fill up most of the space inside your chest. Each lung is enclosed and protected in an airtight lining called a pleural sac. The inside of your chest is also lined with a pleural sac. The linings are smooth and moist. They allow your lungs to move easily within your chest when you breathe. Your left and right lungs are joined together in the center in an area called the hilum. Your left lung is a little smaller than your right lung because your heart is on the left side and takes up space.

The amount of air the lungs can hold is called lung capacity. Lung capacity normally increases until our late teens or early twenties and declines gradually as we age. An average adult has a lung capacity of about twelve pints of air. When resting, a person breathes in and out about ten to fifteen times a minute. With each breath, about a pint of air enters and leaves the lungs. When you exercise, you breathe more quickly and deeply so more air goes in and out of your body every minute.

Have you ever squeezed a rubber bath toy? When you squeeze the toy, the air pushes out. When you release the pressure, the air pushes back in. Your lungs work much the same way.

Your chest is enclosed by your ribs, spinal column, breastbone, and all the muscles in between. The bottom of your chest is enclosed by a strong sheet of muscle and connective tissue called the diaphragm. You inhale when the muscles of your diaphragm pull together and move downward. At the same time, your ribs and breastbone move forward and upward. The movements enlarge the size of your chest cavity. Outside air pushes in through your air tubes to take up the extra room.

A few seconds later the muscles of your diaphragm relax and move upward to their rest position. Your chest muscles also relax, and your ribs and breastbone move backward and downward. Your chest cavity becomes smaller, and there is less room in your lungs. The air is pushed out and you exhale. Even when you breathe out, there is some air still left in your lungs. When you breathe normally, your diaphragm moves up and down only about a half inch. But when you are exercising, your diaphragm may move up and down three or four inches.

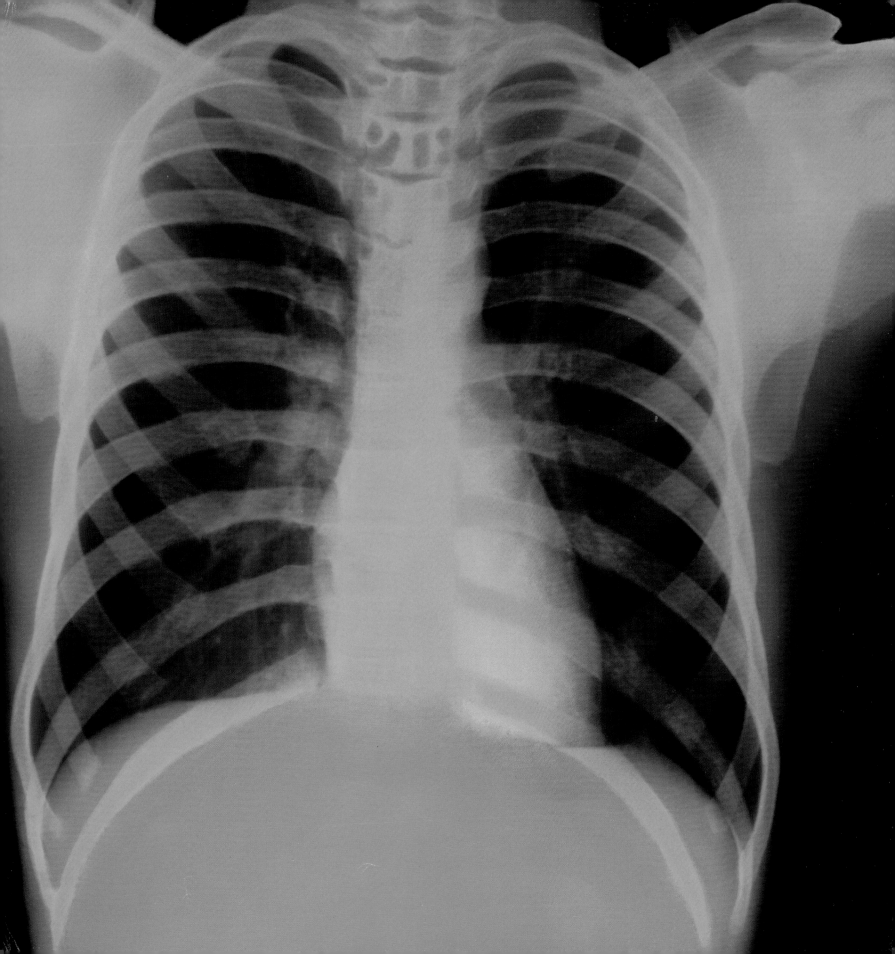

You can control the sounds that air makes as it rushes out of your lungs through your mouth and nose. Place your fingers an inch away from your mouth. Now say this sentence: "Puppies play patty poo." Do you feel the air passing your lips when you talk? When you laugh, you exhale in a series of short breaths. Try it.

When you breathe in deeply and uncontrollably with your mouth open, it's called a yawn. You may yawn if you're bored or tired. Dogs, cats, and other animals yawn, too. No one is sure exactly why we yawn. We're also not sure why we often yawn after we see another person yawn. Did you yawn when you saw the picture on this page?

Some people snore when they sleep. Snoring happens when the throat muscles relax and vibrate, and the airway is partly blocked. Snoring is worse when people sleep on their backs, so sleeping on your side or with a pillow may help. Some people naturally snore a lot and others don't snore much at all.

A sneeze is a sudden burst of exhaled air that comes out of your nose or mouth. It is generally caused by an irritation in the mucus lining. A powerful sneeze pushes air out of your nose or mouth at speeds of up to one hundred miles an hour. Mucus, dust, and germs are carried along with the air and can travel as much as ten feet. Using a tissue when you sneeze helps to prevent your germs from coming into contact with other people.

A cough is an uncontrollable burst of air like a sneeze, but the air only comes out of your mouth. Air rushes out of your lungs and passes over your vocal cords, making a sound. Coughing often occurs to help spit up, or expel, mucus from your airways, so it's a good idea to cough into a tissue just as you use a tissue when you sneeze.

Hiccups are caused by a sudden twitching of your diaphragm that forces air into your lungs. At the same time, the epiglottis flaps snap shut. This sudden closing blocks off the air and produces the hiccup noise. You can try to stop hiccups by holding your breath for a few moments, or taking a long drink of water, or breathing deeply and slowly.

Your lungs and the other parts of your respiratory system can be irritated by dust, smoke, pollen, and infections caused by germs and viruses. An inflammation of your larynx, pharynx, and **tonsils** results in a sore throat. An inflammation of your larynx also makes it difficult to speak, and your voice sounds hoarse. These symptoms usually last only a few days and can be helped by resting and drinking warm liquids. A doctor may prescribe an **antibiotic** to help clear up an infection caused by germs.

These are more serious respiratory problems:

Tonsillitis is an inflammation of the tonsils, caused by a virus or by a germ called *Streptococcus*, or strep.

Bronchitis is an irritation of the lining of the bronchial tubes. People with bronchitis cough a great deal and often are short of breath because of the excess mucus caused by the illness.

Pleurisy is an infection of the pleural sac membranes around the lungs.

Pneumonia is an infection of the air sacs in the lungs.

Tuberculosis (TB) is an infection that damages lung tissue.

Emphysema is a disease in which the lungs become less elastic, often due to years of cigarette smoking.

Many of these conditions require prompt medical attention.

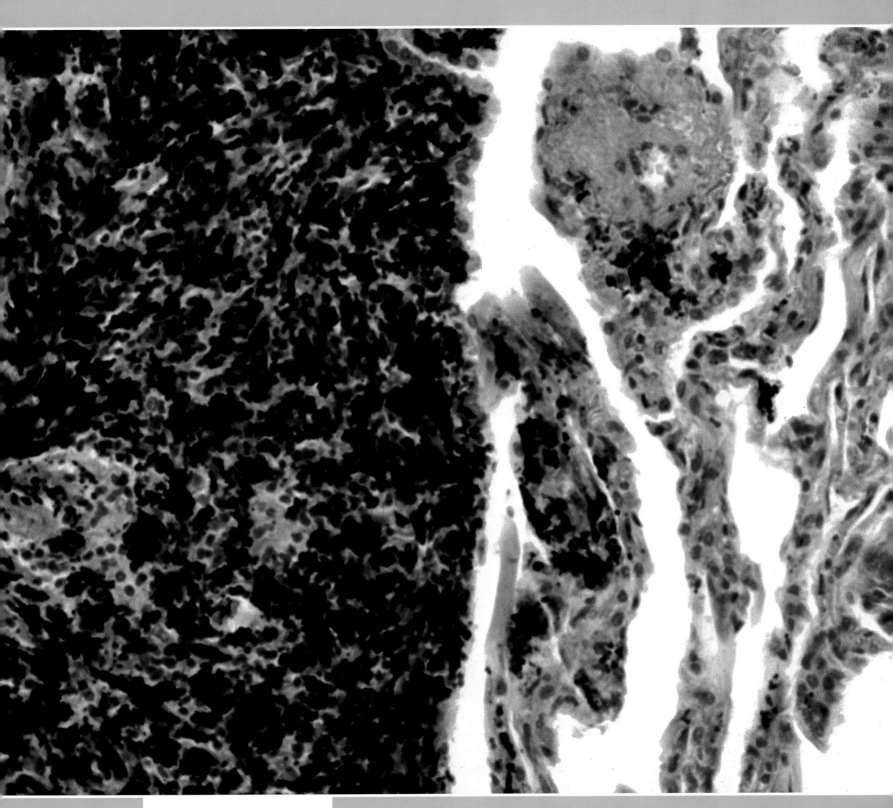

Damaged lungs of a smoker

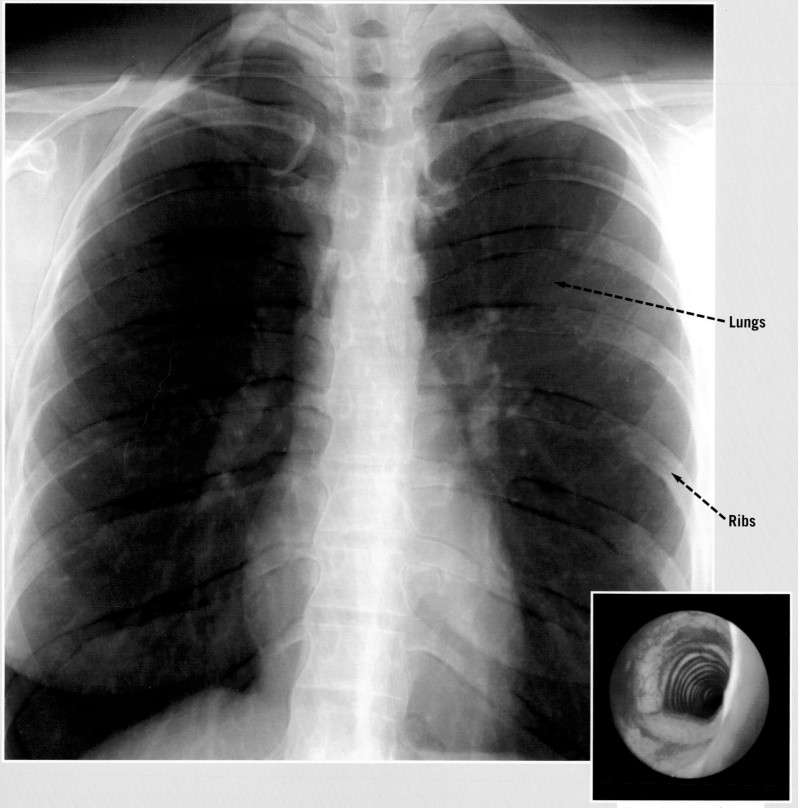

Lungs

Ribs

Bronchoscope image
of a normal trachea

Doctors use a stethoscope to listen to the sounds of a person breathing. For more detailed examinations, doctors use other instruments. A bronchoscope is a flexible tube of glass fibers with a light on the end that acts like a flashlight and a mirror at the same time. It is slipped inside a patient's trachea through the mouth or nose and then into one of the larger bronchial tubes. The doctor is able to shine a light inside and see the inner surface of the airway.

A doctor uses an X-ray to take a picture of the ribs and lungs inside a patient's chest. A diseased or damaged part of a lung shows up as a white shadow on the X-ray photograph. Illnesses such as TB or lung cancer can be detected through the use of X-rays.

During a CAT (computerized axial tomography) scan, X-ray pictures of a patient are taken from many different angles. The images are transmitted to a computer and are often colorized to make them clearer. The photos show the airways and blood vessels inside the lungs and can help a doctor to find the exact location of a problem.

In a quiet place, listen to the sound of your breathing. Each day you inhale and exhale more than twenty thousand times. Awake or asleep, healthy or sick, tired or full of energy, you take one breath after another. From the moment you're born, your lungs and the rest of your respiratory system are always at work.

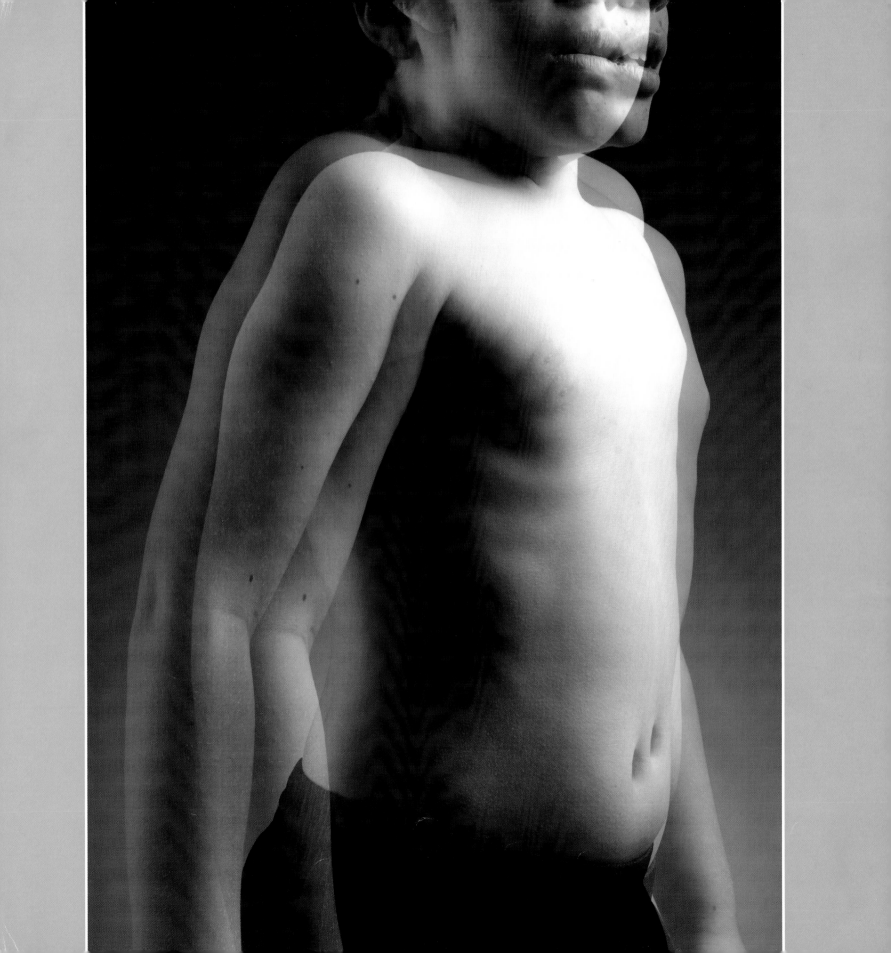

GLOSSARY

Alveoli—Tiny, thin-walled, capillary-rich sacs in the lungs where the exchange of oxygen and carbon dioxide takes place. Alveoli are also called air sacs.

Antibiotic—A substance, such as penicillin, that is produced from certain bacteria and other organisms and is used in the prevention and treatment of infectious diseases.

Capillaries—The smallest blood vessels that form a network throughout the body for the exchange of various substances, such as oxygen and carbon dioxide, between blood and tissue cells.

Cartilage—The tough, elastic, connective tissue that makes up parts of the body such as the joints, outer ear, nose, and larynx.

Cell—The smallest independent unit of an organism that is the building block of all life. A human body contains millions of cells.

Hemoglobin—The protein substance of red blood cells that transports oxygen from the lungs to the tissues of the body.

Membranes—Thin layers of skin that cover surfaces or separate or connect regions, structures, or organs of an animal or a plant.

Molecule—The smallest unit of a substance that still contains all the elements that make up that substance.

Mucus—A sticky and slippery substance that moistens and protects membranes in the nose, throat, and lungs.

Sinus—A long and narrow cavity in the skull that contains air and connects with the nasal cavity.

Tonsils—A pair of tissue masses that protect the body from respiratory infections, located in the walls of the opening between the mouth and pharynx.

INDEX

Bold type indicates illustrations.

READ MORE ABOUT IT

www.si.edu
Smithsonian Institution

www.cancer.org
American Cancer Society

www.lungusa.org
American Lung Association

www.nhlbi.nih.gov
National Heart, Lung, and Blood Institute

AIR IS ALL AROUND YOU
by Franklyn M. Branley

THE BRAIN:
Our Nervous System
by Seymour Simon

A DROP OF BLOOD
by Paul Showers

THE HEART:
Our Circulatory System
by Seymour Simon